ADAPT

Attention Deficit Accommodation Plan for Teaching

PURPOSE OF ADAPT

Children and youth with attention deficit disorders (ADD) often have serious problems in school. Inattention, impulsivity, and hyperactivity can lead to unfinished assignments, careless errors, and behavior which is disruptive to one's self and others. Through the implementation of relatively simple and straightforward accommodations to the classroom environment or teaching style, teachers can adapt to the strengths and weaknesses of students with ADD. Small changes in how a teacher approaches the student with ADD or in what the teacher expects can turn a losing year into a winning one for the student.

On September 16, 1991 the U.S. Department of Education explained its policy on ADD in a memorandum to chief state school officers. Finding ADD to be a serious problem affecting an estimated 2.25 million students (3% - 5%) in our nation's schools, the Department pointed out that students with ADD may require special education services (under IDEA) or accommodations (under Section 504 of the Rehabilitation Act of 1973) to assist them in school if their ability to learn or to otherwise benefit from their education is substantially limited due to their having an attention deficit disorder. While only a relatively small percentage of students with ADD will require special education programming, a much greater number will benefit from accommodations made to the classroom environment or teaching style.

MATERIALS NEEDED FOR ADAPT

The ADD Hyperactivity Handbook for Schools (Parker, 1992) describes characteristics of children with ADD, presumed causes of the disorder, methods of assessment, and discusses accommodations and interventions which teachers can use in the classroom. The *Attention Deficit Accommodation Plan for Teaching (ADAPT)*, is an extension of the ideas in the *Handbook*. Using the ADAPT program, teachers can easily identify ways to modify the classroom environment or their teaching style to fit a student's style of learning and performance. The ADAPT program can be used for elementary and middle school students in conjunction with the *ADAPT Teacher Planbook* and the *ADAPT Student Planbook*.

The *ADAPT Teacher Planbook* guides the teacher in evaluating a student's areas of difficulty leading to the design and implementation of classroom accommodations which may facilitate academic performance and improve social adjustment and self-esteem. Forms found in the Teacher Planbook include: Academic Performance Inventory (API), Accommodation Plan, Accommodation Tracking Form, and Medication Effects Rating Scale (these forms are also sold separately). A set of four teacher planbooks are included in the ADAPT kit to allow for periodic review and tracking of accommodations which may be necessary to implement over the course of the school year.

The *ADAPT Student Planbook* contains record forms to help students plan their assignments and keep track of their daily performance. This planbook also contains worksheets to be used in conjuction with the accommodation plan designed by the teacher. Each student planbook can be used for four to six weeks. A set of four student planbooks are included in the ADAPT kit.

Steps in Using the ADAPT Teacher Planbook and Student Planbook

1. Identify the student's areas of difficulty by completing the Academic Performance Inventory.
2. Write an Accommodation Plan.
3. Complete the Accommodation Plan Tracking Form to monitor student performance.
4. Use the Student Planbook to: help students organize assignments; track students' daily performance; facilitate communication with parents; help students set goals; and implement segments of the Accommodation Plan.

ADAPT Teacher Planbook Copyright ©1992 Specialty Press, Inc. (954) 792-8944 ISBN 1-886941-09-2
All rights reserved.

Using ADAPT Within a Prereferral Intervention Model

In a prereferral intervention model, the design and application of accommodations can be done through a team approach. Such teams (prereferral intervention team, child study team, teacher assistance team, etc.) are frequently made up of the regular education teacher, a school psychologist or school counselor, and a special educator, but can include experts in the area of attention deficit disorders, emotional handicaps or behavioral impairments, behavior management specialists, physicians, psychologists, social workers, reading specialists, etc. One of the members of the team is usually assigned the role of case manager. The case manager has the responsibility of following the student and keeping track of team decisions and the outcome of interventions and procedures used.

For example, a student who has ADD may be brought to the attention of the team by a teacher who is looking for ways to help the student. The team might suggest that the teacher use the ADAPT program to document any areas of difficulty which the student may have and to then design an Accommodation Plan which could help the student. The team might assist the teacher in implementing those classroom accommodations which have been selected to help the student.

Using the Academic Performance Inventory (API) To Identify A Student's Needs*

The Academic Performance Inventory (API) was developed to assist teachers in documenting specific difficulties which are commonly found in the classroom performance of students with ADD. Such difficulties are grouped within eight problem areas:

1. Attention
2. Impulsiveness
3. Motor Activity
4. Organization and Planning
5. Compliance
6. Mood
7. Social Interaction
8. Academic Skills

Each area of difficulty is defined by specific items describing characteristics found in students with ADD. The teacher is instructed to identify if the student in question has had a significant problem relative to most other students in the class in the past two weeks. Behaviors so identified may become targeted for inclusion in the Accommodation Plan.

Writing an Accommodation Plan*

Preparing an Accommodation Plan from the information in the API can be easily accomplished by selecting any number of recommended accommodations relevant to the areas of difficulty specified. Accommodations may result in improved academic performance by the student or in the teacher de-emphasizing those areas of difficulty which the student may be unable to control or improve. Classroom accommodations made for students with ADD may be likened to eyeglasses prescribed for those with vision problems. Neither the accommodations nor the eyeglasses result in a cure, but they may both enable the student to function better. Like eyeglasses, accommodations have to be individually prescribed and periodically revised. Teachers should evaluate the impact of such accommodations on student performance and should be ready to revise the Accommodation Plan as the year progresses.

Tracking Student Performance Under the Accommodation Plan*

Periodic evaluation of student performance under the Accommodation Plan is essential and may be done by the teacher alone or in conjunction with the case manager assigned by the prereferral intervention team. The purpose of such an evaluation is to determine how the plan is working and what modifications, if any, may need to be made. It is recommended that evaluations take place every six to eight weeks (about every reporting period). A parent-teacher conference should be held to discuss the results of the evaluation and all those involved in the student's education should be considered when determining if any changes should be made to the plan or if further steps need to be taken to help the student. Teachers may use the Medication Effects Rating Scale to report medication effects to parents and physicians.

*Academic Performance Inventory, Accommodation Plan, and Accommodation Tracking Form, Medication Effects Rating Scale are also sold separately

Academic Performance Inventory (API)

ADAPT

Name: _____ Grade: _____

Date: _____ School: _____

Completed by:: _____ Case Manager: _____

INSTRUCTIONS: For each of the below items, please check (√) only if the student has had a <u>significant</u> problem relative to most other students in the class <u>in the past two weeks</u>.

In the area of **ATTENTION**, this student:
___ is easily distracted by other students or events
___ has difficulty sustaining attention
___ has difficulty following instructions
___ often does not seem to listen (pay attention)
___ is "spacey"; in own world, often daydreams

In the area of **IMPULSIVENESS**, this student:
___ has difficulty awaiting his/her turn
___ often blurts out
___ shifts excessively from one activity to another
___ has difficulty remaining quiet
___ often rushes through assignments

In the area of **MOTOR ACTIVITY**, this student:
___ has difficulty staying seated
___ fidgets excessively
___ is excessively restless, always on the go
___ is far less active than most others in class
___ works very slowly

In the area of **ORGANIZATION/PLANNING**, this student:
___ has trouble organizing belongings (supplies, books)
___ has trouble organizing and completing classwork
___ has trouble organizing and completing homework
___ has trouble planning short-term projects (up to one week ahead)
___ has trouble planning long-term projects (more than one week ahead)

In the area of **COMPLIANCE**, this student:
___ often loses temper
___ often argues with adults
___ often actively defies or refuses adult requests or rules

___ often blames others for own mistakes
___ is often touchy or easily annoyed by others
___ is overly passive
___ excessively submissive to others

In the area of **MOOD**, this student:
___ worries excessively
___ shows marked self-consciousness
___ often needs reassurance
___ has a marked inability to relax
___ exhibits feelings of worthlessness or excessive guilt
___ is easily frustrated, gives up easily
___ often becomes angry and loses temper
___ frequently withdraws from others
___ frequently gets into fights

In the area of **SOCIAL INTERACTION**, this student:
___ acts in an overly dominating manner with peers
___ gets too excitable; overwhelms classmates
___ does not pay attention to important social cues
___ overreacts to minor events
___ argues with peers
___ misperceives actions of others as being hostile
___ teases or is overly critical of others
___ is excessively shy, quiet
___ is very passive, submissive
___ withdraws from others

In the area of **ACADEMIC SKILLS**, this student:
___ has problems reading
___ has problems with math
___ has problems with spelling
___ has problems communicating with written language
___ has problems with oral communication
___ other_____

This inventory was designed for descriptive purposes only and has not been norm-referenced.

©1992 Specialty Press, Inc. (954) 792-8944 ADAPT Program All Rights Reserved

Accommodation Plan

ADAPT

Name: _____ Grade: _____

Date: _____ School: _____

Completed by: _____ Case Manager: _____

INSTRUCTIONS: Consider the student's areas of difficulty noted on the Academic Performance Inventory (API). Check the accommodations which will be implemented to adapt to the student's areas of difficulty.

1. ATTENTION
___ seat student in quiet area (1.1)
___ seat student near good role model (1.2)
___ seat student near "study buddy" (1.3)
___ increase distance between desks (1.4)
___ seat student away from distracting stimuli (1.5)
___ allow extra time to complete assigned work (1.6)
___ shorten assignments/work periods; use timer (1.7)
___ break long assignments into smaller parts (1.8)
___ assist student in setting short-term goals (1.9)
___ give assignments one at a time (1.10)
___ require fewer correct responses for grade (1.11)
___ reduce amount of homework (1.12)
___ provide instuction in self-monitoring using cueing (1.13)
___ pair written instructions with oral instructions (1.14)
___ provide peer assistance in notetaking (1.15)
___ give clear, concise instructions (1.16)
___ increase saliency of lesson to student (1.17)
___ look at student when talking (1.18)
___ seek to involve student in lesson presentation (1.19)
___ provide written outline of lesson (1.20)
___ pair students to check work (1.21)
___ cue student to stay on task, i.e. private signal (1.22)
___ other_____ (1.23)
___ other_____ (1.24)

2. IMPULSIVENESS
___ ignore minor, inappropriate behavior (2.1)
___ increase immediacy of rewards or consequences (2.2)
___ use time-out procedure for misbehavior (2.3)
___ supervise closely during transition times (2.4)
___ use "prudent" reprimands for misbehavior (i.e. avoid lecturing or criticism) (2.5)
___ attend to positive behavior with praise, etc. (2.6)
___ acknowledge good behavior of other students (2.7)
___ seat student near good role model or teacher (2.8)
___ set up behavior contract (2.9)
___ instruct student in self-monitoring of behavior, i.e. hand raising, calling out (2.10)
___ call on only when hand is raised appropriately (2.11)
___ ignore calling out without raising hand (2.12)
___ praise student when hand raised (2.13)
___ implement behavior management system (2.14)
___ implement home-school token system (2.15)
___ other_____ (2.16)
___ other_____ (2.17)

3. MOTOR ACTIVITY
___ allow student to stand at times while working (3.1)
___ provide opportunity for "seat breaks" (3.2)
___ provide short break between assignments (3.3)
___ supervise closely during transition times (3.4)
___ remind student to check over work product (3.5)
___ give extra time to complete tasks (especially for students with slow motor tempo) (3.6)
___ other_____ (3.7)
___ other_____ (3.8)

4. ORGANIZATION and PLANNING
___ request parental help with organization (4.1)
___ provide rules for getting organized (4.2)
___ encourage student to have notebook with dividers and folders for work (4.3)
___ provide homework assignment book (4.4)
___ supervise writing of homework assignments (4.5)
___ check homework daily (4.6)
___ send daily/weekly progress reports home (4.7)
___ check desk/notebook for neatness, encourage neatness rather than penalize sloppiness (4.8)
___ allow student to have extra set books at home (4.9)
___ provide peer assistance with organization (4.10)
___ give assignments one at a time (4.11)
___ set short-term goals in completing assignments (4.12)
___ do not penalize for handwriting if visual-motor deficits or organizational deficits present (4.13)
___ encourage learning of keyboarding skills (4.14)
___ allow tape recording of assignments (4.15)
___ write main points of lessons on chalkboard (4.16)
___ use visual aids in lesson presentation (4.17)
___ other_____ (4.18)
___ other_____ (4.19)

©1992 Specialty Press, Inc. (954) 792-8944 ADAPT Program All Rights Reserved

Accommodation Plan (continued)

5. COMPLIANCE
___ praise compliant behavior (5.1)
___ post class rules in conspicuous place (5.2)
___ provide immediate feedback about behavior (5.3)
___ ignore minor inappropriate behavior (5.4)
___ use teacher attention to praise positive actions (5.5)
___ use "prudent" reprimands for misbehavior (i.e. avoid lecturing or criticism) (5.6)
___ acknowledge good behavior of nearby student (5.7)
___ supervise closely during transition times (5.8)
___ seat student near good role models or teacher (5.9)
___ set up behavior contract (5.10)
___ implement behavior management system (5.11)
___ instruct student in self-monitoring, i.e. following directions, raise hand to talk (5.12)
___ other_____ (5.13)
___ other_____ (5.14)

6. MOOD
___ provide reassurance and encouragement (6.1)
___ compliment positive behavior and work (6.2)
___ speak softly in nonthreatening manner if student shows nervousness (6.3)
___ review instructions for new assignments to make sure student comprehends (6.4)
___ look for opportunities for student to display leadership role in class (6.5)
___ focus on student's talents/accomplishments (6.6)
___ conference frequently with parents to learn about student's interests and achievements (6.7)
___ send positive notes home (6.8)
___ assign student to be a peer teacher (6.9)
___ make time to talk alone with student (6.10)
___ encourage social interactions with classmates if student is withdrawn or excessively shy (6.11)
___ reinforce frequently when signs of frustration are noticed (6.12)
___ look for signs of stress build up and provide encouragement or reduced work load (6.13)
___ spend more time talking to students who seem pent up or display anger easily (6.14)
___ train anger control: encourage student to walk away; use calming strategies (6.15)
___ other_____ (6.16)
___ other_____ (6.17)

7. SOCIALIZATION
___ praise appropriate social behavior (7.1)
___ monitor social interactions to gain clearer sense of student's behavior with others (7.2)
___ set up social behavior goals with student and implement a reward program (7.3)
___ prompt appropriate social behavior either verbally or with private signal (7.4)
___ encourage student to observe classmate who exhibits appropriate social skills (7.5)
___ avoid placing student in competitive activities (7.6)
___ encourage cooperative learning tasks (7.7)
___ provide small group social skills training in-class or through related services (7.8)
___ praise student to increase esteem to others (7.9)
___ assign special responsibilities to student in presence of peers to elevate status in class (7.10)
___ other_____ (7.11)
___ other_____ (7.12)

8. ACADEMIC SKILL
___ if skill weaknesses are suspected refer for academic achievement assessment (8.1)
___ if reading is weak: provide additional reading time; use "previewing" strategies; select text with less on a page; shorten amount of required reading; avoid oral reading (8.2)
___ if oral expression is weak: accept all oral responses; substitute display for oral report; encourage expression of new ideas or experiences; pick topics easy for student to talk about (8.3)
___ if written language is weak: accept non-written forms for reports (i.e. displays, oral, projects); accept use of typewriter, word processor, tape recorder; do not assign large quantity of written work; test with multiple choice or fill-in questions; instruction in "brain storming" to generate ideas (8.4)
___ if math is weak: allow use of calculator; use graph paper to space numbers; provide additional math time; provide immediate correctness feedback and instruction via modeling of the correct computational procedure; teach the steps needed to solve a particular math problem; give clues to the process needed to solve problem; encourage use of "self-talk" to proceed through problem-solving (8.5)
___ other_____ (8.6)
___ other_____ (8.7)

9. OTHER ACCOMMODATIONS
___ schedule regular parent-teacher conferences (9.1)
___ consult with outside professionals, i.e. counselor, psychologist, educational tutor, etc. as needed (9.2)
___ establish procedure for dispensing medication (9.3)
___ assist physician in monitoring of behavior and attention when medication is taken (9.4)
___ monitor medication side-effects (9.5)
___ suggest group/individual counseling (9.6)
___ recommend parenting program(s) (9.7)
___ alert bus driver as to student's needs (9.8)
___ suggest other agency involvement _____ (9.9)
___ suggest parents attend parent support group (9.10)
___ other_____ (9.11)
___ other_____ (9.12)

©1992 Specialty Press, Inc. (954) 792-8944 ADAPT Program All Rights Reserved

Accommodation Tracking Form

ADAPT

Name:	Jonathan Evans	Grade:	Fifth
Date:	11/5/92	School:	Hawthorne Elementary
Completed by:	Mrs. Morgan	Case Manager:	Mrs. Fielding, Guidance

AREA(S) OF DIFFICULTY (Refer to API)	ACCOMMODATION(S) IMPLEMENTED (Refer to Accommodation Plan)	DATE STARTED	RESULT
1. Is easily distracted; has difficulty staying on task	• seat student in quiet area (1.1) • seat student near good role model (1.2) • assist student in setting short term goals (1.9) • require fewer correct answers (1.11) • cue student to stay on task (1.22)	10/1/92	improvement in amount of classrwork done student seems less frustrated
2. often blurts out	• ignore minor, inappropriate behavior (2.1) • attend to positive behavior (2.6) • instruct student in self-monitoring using hand-raising self-monitoring form (2.1)	10/1/92	less calling out student catching self more often
3. rushes through assignments	• remind student to check over work (3.5)	10/1/92	student taking more time to finish work
4. often loses temper	• focus on student's accomplishments (6.6) • make time to talk alone with student (6.10) • look for signs of stress build up and provide encouragement (6.13)	10/1/92	no change...student still gets frustrated easily
5. has trouble organizing and completing homework	• request parental help with organization at home (4.1) • encourage use of notebook dividers (4.3) • provide homework assignment book (4.4) • check homework daily (4.6)	10/1/92	homework coming in better notebook better organized

©1992 Specialty Press, Inc. (954) 792-8944 ADAPT Program All Rights Reserved

ADAPT

Accommodation Tracking Form

Name:

Date:

Completed by:

Grade:

School:

Case Manager:

AREA(S) OF DIFFICULTY (Refer to API)	ACCOMMODATION(S) IMPLEMENTED (Refer to Accommodation Plan)	DATE STARTED	RESULT

©1992 Specialty Press, Inc. (954) 792-8944 ADAPT Program All Rights Reserved

Medication Effects Rating Scale

Name: _____   Grade: _____

Date: _____   School: _____

Completed By: _____   Physician: _____

List name(s) of medication student is taking:

MEDICATION(S)	DOSAGE(S)	TIME(S) OF DAY TAKEN	DISPENSED BY
_____	_____	_____	_____
_____	_____	_____	_____
_____	_____	_____	_____

Mark any changes noticed in the following behaviors:

Behavior	Worse	No Change	Improved A Little	Improved A Lot
attention to task	____	____	____	____
listening to lessons	____	____	____	____
finishing work	____	____	____	____
impulsiveness	____	____	____	____
calling out in class	____	____	____	____
organization, fine motor	____	____	____	____
overactivity	____	____	____	____
restlessness, fidgety	____	____	____	____
talkativeness	____	____	____	____
aggressiveness	____	____	____	____

Mark any side effects noticed by you or mentioned by student:

Side Effects	Comments
appetite loss	_____
insomnia	_____
headaches	_____
stomach aches	_____
seems tired	_____
stares a lot	_____
irritable	_____
vocal or motor tic	_____
sadness	_____
nervousness	_____

©1992 Specialty Press, Inc. (954) 792-8944 ADAPT Program All Rights Reserved

Information Regarding
Section 504 of the Rehabilitation Act of 1973

Section 504 is an Act which prohibits discrimination against persons with a handicap in any program receiving Federal financial assistance. The Act defines a person with a handicap as anyone who:

1. has a mental or physical impairment which substantially limits one or more major life activities (major life activities include activities such as caring for one's self, performing manual tasks, walking, seeing, hearing, speaking, breathing, learning and working);
2. has a record of such an impairment; or
3. is regarded as having such an impairment.

In order to fulfill its obligation under Section 504, school districts recognize a responsibility to avoid discrimination in policies and practices regarding their personnel and students. No discrimination of any person with a handicap will knowingly be permitted in any of the programs and practices in school systems.

School districts have specific responsibilities under the Act, which include the responsibility to identify, evaluate, and if the child is determined to be eligible under Section 504, to afford access to appropriate educational services.

If the parent or guardian disagrees with the determination made by the professional staff of a school district, he/she has a right to a hearing with an impartial hearing officer.

The Family Educational Rights and Privacy Act (FERPA) also specifies rights related to educational records. This Act gives the parent or guardian the right to: 1) inspect and review his/her child's educational records; 2) make copies of these records; 3) receive a list of all individuals having access to those records; 4) ask for an explanation of any item in the records; 5) ask for an amendment to any report on the grounds that it is inaccurate, misleading, or violates the child's rights; and 6) a hearing on the issue if the school refuses to make the amendment.

For the Teacher
Using the Student Planbook

Purpose of the Student Planbook

The Student Planbook contains a variety of forms which may be used by the student alone or together with his/her teacher(s) and parent(s) to provide training in areas related to planning of academic work, organization, goal setting, self-monitoring of attention and behavior, behavior modification, and the use of appropriate social skills. These recording forms and activity sheets have been found to be helpful with elementary school-aged students with attentional problems, however, many portions of the planbook are suitable for any student who needs additional structure in school. All pages in the planbook (except for the Daily Record Form) may be reproduced for the student's personal use *only* and are perforated for easy accessibility. A fuller explanation of these forms can be found in *The ADD Hyperactivity Handbook for Schools* by Harvey C. Parker, Ph.D.*

Introducing the Planbook to the Student and Parents

The Student Planbook should be introduced to both the student and his/her parents together. Activity sheets in the planbook will generally be regarded as "fun" by students, therefore, avoid any implication that the student is using the planbook as a penalty for poor performance or problematic behavior or as a sign that s/he is "different" from others in the class.

Skim through the planbook with the student and parents. Direct the student to keep the planbook in his/her looseleaf notebook and to bring it to school and home each day. Next, instruct the student in how to fill out the Planner for the Month, Class Directory, and the Daily Record Form. Spend additional time going over other sections of the planbook as needed and discuss with the student and parents how to best use these forms throughout the school year.

Using the Daily Record Form

Carefully review the Daily Record Form during the initial meeting with the student and parents. This form can be used as an assignment journal (to be completed by the student) and/or as a classroom performance report for students at or above the second grade level (to be completed by the teacher). The Daily Record Form should not be removed from the planbook. Multiple copies are provided. An easier version of this form is supplied for use with students in kindergarten and first grade and should be reproduced for daily use.

As an assignment journal, space is provided for the student to write down daily assignments. Icons indicate supplies needed to be brought home to complete work. Long-term projects and tests should be noted on the Monthly Planner. The teacher(s) may choose to review and initial that the student copied all assignments correctly.

The "Score Board", part of the Daily Record Form, is a home-school based token program which targets five behaviors commonly found to be problematic for students with attentional difficulties. The teacher rates the student on a five point scale (1= Poor to 5=Excellent). When a category of behavior does not apply for the student for that day, i.e. no homework assigned, the teacher(s) mark N/A and the student is automatically awarded 5 points. Emphasize to both the student and the parents that the student's behavior will be rated *every* day (perhaps more than once per day) and that it is essential for the parents to review these ratings at home and discuss the student's progress as needed. Encouragement should be offered to the child by the parents in the form of verbal praise and tangible rewards for his or her successes while loss of privileges may be applied for point totals below a prescribed amount each day (to be determined by parents and teacher). Explain to the child that if s/he does not bring the planbook to school for daily scoring s/he will be give zero points for the day and appropriate consequences would follow.

When setting up the rewards and consequences for the student, be careful to establish cut-off scores at a realistic level so that the student can be successful provided that a reasonable effort is made. Although individual differences need to be considered, we have found that a score of 17 points per rating period (AM, PM, Once a Day) is an effective cut-off score for starting the program. If the student receives less than the cut-off number of points on any given day then a mild consequence should be provided at home or in school, however, for points at or above the amount expected a reward should be forthcoming.

The combined use of rewards and negative consequences provides the initial motivation to the student to succeed. When the program is working well and the student consistently brings home good marks on the "Score Board" s/he gains a sense of pride about their performance. The joy of a job well done becomes an even more powerful incentive to the child than extrinisic rewards or negative consequences. Gradually daily ratings can be spaced out as the student's behavior indicates that fading out of the program is warranted.

Using the Self-Monitoring Activity Sheets

Self-monitoring is an effective treatment procedure for helping children with attentional disorders in school settings. In self-monitoring, children are trained to observe specific aspects of their own behavior and to record their observations. For example, a child who calls out a great deal may be asked to observe whenever s/he asks for permission to speak and is trained to record each time s/he does so. Self-monitoring has been used in the classroom to help children pay attention, complete academic assignments, improve speed of classroom performance, control behavior, etc.. Such an approach is popular with teachers because it is self-administered by the student and takes little teacher time.

A number of self-monitoring activity sheets can be found in the Student Planbook:
- *I Can Do It*
- *Getting Along*
- *Hand Raising Record Form*
- *Writing Reminders*
- *Proofreading Checklist*
- *Homework Self-Check*
- *Was I Paying Attention* (requires the use of an audio "beep" tape; see below*)

Using the Contracts and Point Progams

A behavioral contract is an agreement drawn up between two or more parties, in this case a teacher, a parent, and a student, wherein the student agrees to behave in a specified manner in exhcange for some specific reciprocal behavior from the teacher or parent. The purpose of the contract is to restructure the environment to provide a consistent set of expectations and consequences to the student, based upon certain pre-defined performance criteria. Behavioral contracts have been used successfully for many years to motivate students to perform. Contracts are often successful because they provide a "win-win" approach to helping the student and take into consideration the personal goals of each party.

Two behavioral contract templates are included in the planbook, one for general behavior and academic performance and the other specifically for homework. Contracting with students who have attentional problems may require the teacher or parent to emphasize immediacy of reinforcement. Non-ADD youngsters are more likely able to wait a day or longer to "cash-in" on their positive performance as per the terms of their behavioral contracts. Many students with attentional problems will probably need more opportunities to receive reinforcement.

*Teachers and parents should consult *The ADD Hyperactivity Handbook for Schools* by Harvey C. Parker Ph.D. for a more detailed explanation of how to use materials found in the Student Planbook. This and the *Listen, Look and Think Program* (endless audio beep tape) are available through the ADD WareHouse • 800 ADD-WARE.

What's Up with Altitude

Mr. Moffat's Class Investigates How Altitude Affects our Bodies

By Lisa Gardiner

The Colorado Mountain Club Press
Golden, Colorado

PUBLISHED IN THE UNITED STATES BY:
The Colorado Mountain Club Press
710 10th St., Suite 200
Golden, CO 80401
(303) 996-2743
Email: cmcpress@cmc.org
Website www.cmc.org

All rights reserved. No part of this publication may be reproduced or transmitted in any form or by any means, electronic or mechanical, including photocopy, recording, or an information storage and retrieval system, without permission in writing from the publisher.

Managing Editor: Gretchen Hanisch
Graphic Design and Layout: Tom Beckwith, Gretchen Hanisch and Lisa Gardiner
Proofing: Gretchen Hanisch
Illustrator: Lisa Gardiner

What's Up with Altitude
By Lisa Gardiner
Library of Congress Control Number: 2004114555
ISBN Number: 0-9724413-8-7

SCFD
Scientific & Cultural Facilities District
Making It Possible.

We gratefully acknowledge the financial support of the citizens of Colorado through the Scientific and Cultural Facilities District for the publication of this book.
Printed in Canada

Thanks so much to Anne Pharamond, Gretchen Hanisch and Teresa Eastburn for comments and encouragement about drafts of text and illustrations. Thanks to Peggy LeMone for taking the time to explain the funny things that molecules do at altitude. This book was inspired by the fantastic programs for kids at the Colorado Mountain Club Youth Education Program which I had the pleasure to develop and teach with talented educators Brenda Porter, Stacey Norman, and Ford Church.

Abby Brittlefern had climbed mountains all over the world. Now she was visiting Denver Elementary to share what it was like to be a mountaineer. What Abby didn't know was that Mr. Moffat's class knew a thing or two about what it was like to be on high mountains.

Abby told them all about her experiences while traveling, and what it feels like to reach the top of a mountain. Some of her stories were a little scary, but all of them were exciting.

"If I wanted to climb the tallest mountains of the world, like Mount Everest," wondered Marty aloud, "what would I need to do?" Many other members of the class, who were fooling around with the climbing gear, paused and listened with interest for Abby's answer.

"If you want to climb high mountains, you have to be prepared.," said Abby. "You will need to learn mountaineering skills, be in good shape, and pack the right supplies," she continued in a wise tone. "But also," she paused dramatically, "to climb mountains safely you need to know what's up with **altitude**."

Giggles throughout the room told Abby that there was something funny about what she had said. "What's so funny about **altitud**e?" she asked in a flustered tone.

"There is nothing funny about it," said Monique while scowling at her giggling classmates, "it's just that we already know all about **altitude**."

"Yeah. It's one of Mr. Moffat's favorite subjects," blurted Zachary stifling a chuckle, "so, we've been learning about it since the second grade."

"How far you are above the sea is called **altitude**. Have a seat and we can tell you all about it," said Grace knowledgeably while pushing a chair from the side of the classroom for Abby to sit in.

"You see," said Mr. Moffat to Abby, as he pulled the rolled map of Colorado down in front of the blackboard, "we are in Colorado!" The map snapped and rolled itself up; the room erupted in laughter.

Mr. Moffat adjusted his tie, pulled down the map and tried again, "This is a state with high **altitudes**! The lowest place in Colorado is about 3,350 feet above sea level and the highest mountaintop is 14,433 feet above sea level. People who live in a place like this have **clues** all around them to how air affects people and things at **altitude**. Now, who has a clue to share about how air and **altitude** affect us?"

Clue #1: What Is Air?

Sam's Balloon and the Power of Air,
–by Marty

"I can't believe my mom made me take my little brother Sam to the Halloween carnival. I knew he'd get all scared and cry, and I'd have to take him out of the haunted house and not get to see the whole thing. And, the haunted house this year was one of the best ones ever. At least that's what my neighbor Justin had said." "Marty," interrupted Mr. Moffat, " what does this have to do with air?"

"Oh, yeah," said Marty, realizing that the whole class was staring at him. "It's part of the story, really."

"Sam is only three years old he's still pretty much a big baby. He even started crying because his balloon was blue and not red. I thought he would probably make it through the whole thing as long as I kept him behind me with his head in my wizard's cloak.

"After standing in the line for a really long time, we finally got to go in. Justin was right. It was really scary and really cool. Sam stayed behind me the whole way. I was looking for the most gruesome stuff I could find. Then, just as I passed a bunch of vampires…BANG…

"…there was a huge noise right behind me; it scared me so much, I dove to the floor. Looking around, the group of Vampires and everyone else did the same thing. Except for Sam, who was just standing there holding the limp piece of blue rubber that had, up until a few seconds before, been his balloon. There may have only been air in there, but it was a powerful thing!"

According to Mr. Moffat...
Air Is Everywhere!

"Excellent story Marty. Ok everyone, let's go outside and take a look around. What do you see?"

"Blue sky, mountains, grassy plains, an earthworm," called students.

"What you are not seeing, however, is air!" said Mr. Moffat in a triumphant voice.

"Air may not seem like much, but it's really there, all around you, not just inside balloons like Sam's. When air moves around, we call it wind. Indoors and outdoors, there is air everywhere you go on the Earth's surface except underwater. It forms a layer around our planet called the **atmosphere**.

"Air is made of tiny particles. In fact, everything is made of tiny particles. These particles are called **molecules** and they are too small to see on their own. They are even too small to see with a microscope. But when many of them are together, they make up the mountains, the clouds, your pets, and even you!

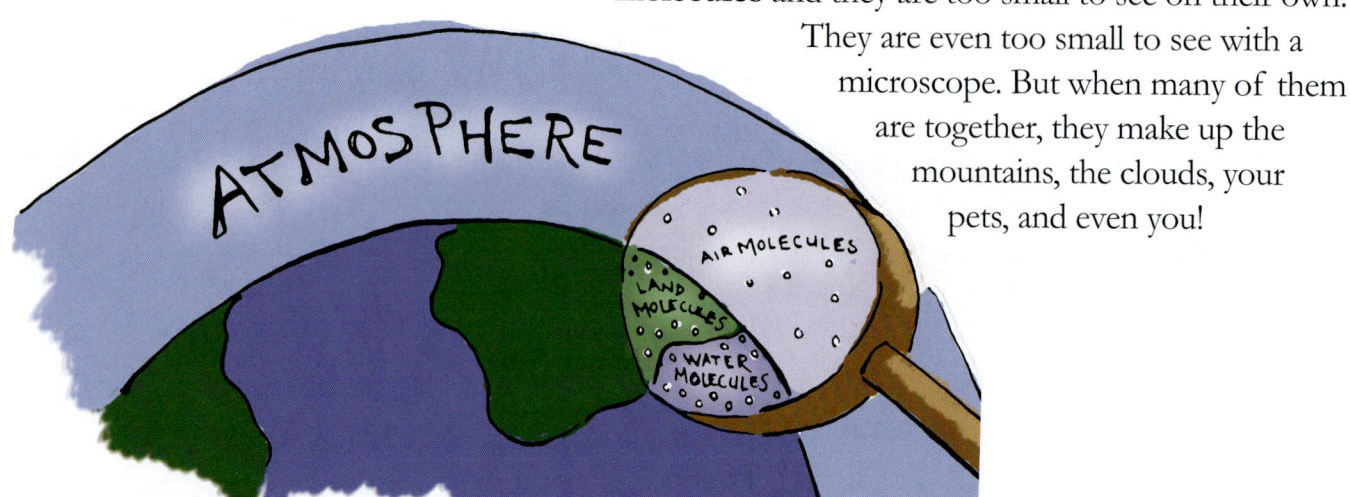

"Since we can't see them, let's pretend that the balls in this gym closet are **molecules**."

"Ahhh!!!" yelled everyone in the class as the gym closet door flew open and balls sprung out everywhere. "My goodness! They were packed in there tightly now weren't they," giggled Abby Brittlefern.

Mr. Moffat, who had nearly fallen over when the tower of balls was released from the closet, caught his breath, cleared his throat and continued as the balls bounced all over the room.

"The **molecules** in air are not all the same type. Over three quarters of them are **molecules** called **nitrogen**. Let's pretend those are the green balls," he said. "Most of the rest are **molecules** called **oxygen**. Let's pretend those are the orange balls. There are small amounts of other stuff too."

Air Is Really There!

TRY IT!

Of course, air is not really made of balls from the gym closet. It is made of little particles called **molecules** that you can't see. Would you like some proof that air is really made of these little things? Try this experiment and see for yourself!

Have you ever tried to balance a seesaw? If the people on either end are made of the same amount of stuff, then the board will balance in the middle. If the two people on the seesaw are very different sizes, then the board will not balance. To balance the seesaw, more of the board's length will need to be at the end with the smaller person.

You can figure out that air is really there by making a seesaw for air! Try this activity to find the point where a small seesaw balances when a container full of air is at one end and a container that has no air is at the other end. If air was made of nothing, then the containers should balance in the same place whether or not one is full of air!

Lighter

Heavier

BALANCED!

What you'll need:

- Two balloons
- Two rubber bands
- Ruler
- Plastic knife
- Lump of play dough

1. Stick the knife handle into the play dough and orient it so that the knife lies on the table on its long edge with the cutting edge pointing up.

2. Attach a balloon to each end of the ruler using a rubber band (or masking tape). It is important that the balloons have no air in them and are not hanging from the ruler. You can wad each up into a ball and attach it to the ruler.

3. Place the ruler on the edge of the plastic knife so that it looks like a seesaw. Move the ruler until it is in a location along the knife where it balances so that neither end of the ruler is touching the table. It may only balance for a second or two.

4. Write down the number of inches or centimeters along the ruler where it touched the knife when balanced.

5. Now remove one of the balloons from the ruler and blow it up, tying the end so that the air stays inside, and reattaching it to the ruler with the rubber band. Remember to attach it in the same spot at the end of the ruler where it was before.

6. Place the ruler back on the knife-edge at the mark where it balanced before. Does the ruler still balance? If not, which end is heavier?

13

Clue #2: Air Pressure and Altitude

The Potato Chip Miracle
–by Grace

"We were on our way up to the mountains for a week of camping. Mom, Jane, Allen, and I were packed into the car with so much stuff that we could hardly see each other over the sleeping bags, tents, and tons of food. We were going to our favorite campground; it is by a lake that is so high up in the mountains, we can usually see snow on the high peaks, even in July.

"I was so excited to go, but I was also hungry. Since I was stuffed in a car full of food, I thought it would be a good time for a snack. I peered into the back to see what was in the boxes of food and spotted a bag of potato chips. "No snacking," said Mom. I grumbled and let go of the chip bag."

"When will we get there," "I asked my mom as the car wound along a mountain road. She said it would only be about half an hour. That can seem like a really long time if you are hungry and are really close to a bag of potato chips that you are not supposed to open. I could see the bag sticking out of the cardboard box full of food. I must have been really hungry because every time I looked into the back, the bag looked as if it had grown bigger and bigger.

"I took one more glance at them and wished silently for some sort of miracle that would let me eat all the chips I wanted. All of a sudden there was an enormous popping noise. Potato chips flew everywhere. I don't know how it happened, but I'm so thankful for the potato chip miracle."

According to Mr. Moffat...
Air Pressure Changes As You Go Up Higher!

"I'm not sure that was a miracle, Grace," said Mr. Moffat grinning. "That was just changing air pressure."

"Remember a few minutes ago when the balls were all packed in the gym closet? They were packed closely together just like air **molecules** are at low **altitudes**. At higher **altitudes**, the **molecules** spread further apart, just like the balls released from the closet.

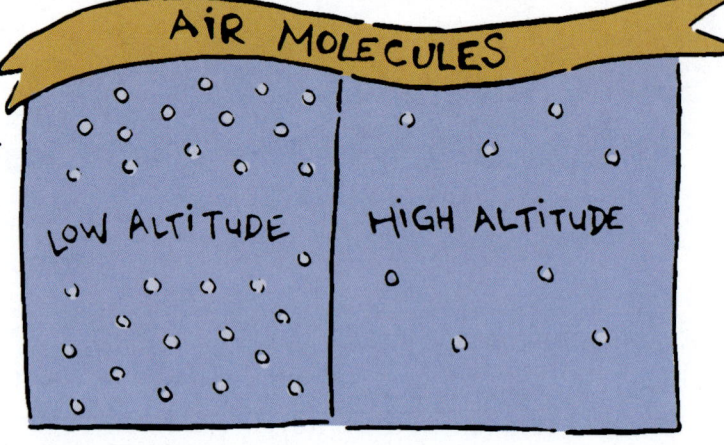

"Why are the **molecules** packed closely together at low **altitudes**? Tilt your head, look up, and think about the huge amount of tiny air **molecules** that are above you. All this air is pushing down on you thanks to the force of **gravity**, which pulls everything towards the earth. People and animals don't notice that the air above is pushing down on them because they are used to it. The weight of all that air is called **air pressure**.

16

"Those air **molecules** are not just pushing down on you, they are also pushing each other so that air **molecules** lower in the **atmosphere** are packed closely together. This is called high **air pressure**. Air **molecules** high up in the **atmosphere** are more spread out because there is low **air pressure**. This means that as you hike or drive to the mountains, you are entering areas with less air **molecules** and lower **air pressure**."

"So at low **altitude** the pressure is high?" frowned Amanda.

"And at high **altitude** the pressure is low?" pondered Zachary.

"That's right," smiled Mr. Moffat, "and it explains why the potato chip bag burst! If a chip bag is sealed shut, the chips are not the only things trapped inside it! Air **molecules** inside it are also trapped. If you take the bag into a place with lower **air pressure**, the air **molecules** inside the bag spread out and the bag inflates. It might even pop open if the bag isn't strong enough to hold the air and can not stretch larger!"

Make An Altimeter To Take Up The Mountains!

TRY iT!

Measure **air pressure** to figure out your **altitude** with an altimeter! This is a great activity to do on a day when you are going to the mountains. Make the altimeter right before you leave your home and watch it as you travel up to the mountains to turn a dull car ride into a science experiment.

What you'll need:

- A small coffee can
- A piece of plastic wrap
- A pair of scissors
- A drinking straw
- An index card
- A rubber band
- Tape

1. Cover the top of the can with plastic wrap and secure it with a rubber band to hold the plastic wrap in place making the can airtight.

2. Lay the straw horizontally on top of the plastic wrap so part of the straw sticks over one side of the can and tape the straw in place.

3. Attach the index card to the can with tape. Make sure it is standing up directly behind the straw.

4. Mark the location of the straw on the index card and write the time of day and location next to your mark.

5. Get into the car and bring your altimeter with you. Record where the straw is against the index card every so often. Remember to write the time and location next to your mark each time. What happens to your barometer when you take it to the mountains? Can you use your barometer to figure out the **altitude**?

What's going on?

High pressure at low **altitudes** will make the plastic wrap cave in, and the straw go up.

Low pressure at high **altitudes** will make the plastic wrap puff up, and the straw go down.

The altimeter is sensitive to temperature as well as **air pressure**, so try to keep temperature the same if you can.

An altimeter is also a barometer, an instrument that meteorologists use to measure how pressure changes because of changes in weather.

HIGH PRESSURE

LOW PRESSURE

Clue #3:
Low Air Pressure Makes It Cold!

It Was Freezing Up There
–by Luis

"I was mostly asleep one spring morning, listening to my alarm clock which was shouting that blue skies and warm weather would fill the day, when my pesky little brother ran into my room, without knocking, yelling something about skiing. He was wearing his long underwear and a helmet and looked completely ridiculous. I had always thought that he was crazy but now I was sure. That is, until dad came into my room tossed my long underwear at me and asked me to give him a hand putting their skis and my snowboard in the car."

"But," I said, "It's too warm for skis and snowboards and way too warm for long underwear." "Not where we are going!" sang dad brightly.

"Are we driving to winter?" I grumbled. "But I climbed out of bed and followed him out of the room anyway. Snowboarding is so much fun, but I thought it was way too warm for winter sports now.

"I was still pretty sleepy when dad sang, 'We're here!' from the front seat of the car after driving into the mountains."

"Fine," I mumbled sleepily and, with my eyes still closed, I opened the car door.

"Eek! I shouted, instantly awake and totally confused, "It's freezing out there! Could we really have driven back into winter?"

"Well, not really," chuckled dad, "it's just the **altitude**."

According to Mr. Moffatt...
It's Chilly When Air Pressure Is Low!

"Excellent point Luis," said Mr. Moffatt. "It may be so warm that you are wearing shorts and eating ice cream, but the top of a nearby high mountain is probably much cooler. It may even be capped with snow."

"But why was it so cold?" asked Luis, " and why did my dad say that it was the **altitude**?"

"You see," replied Mr. Moffatt, "weather in mountain areas can be difficult to predict. Storms can become trapped in the mountains and drop loads of snow in winter. But another reason that you see snow on mountaintops is that it is colder at higher **altitudes** than lower ones.

"Temperature is a measure of how quick the **molecules** move around. At higher **altitudes**, air **molecules** move around quickly bumping into each other because they have energy.

"Since air is always moving, **molecules** at low **altitude** might find themselves at high **altitude** and push apart because of the lower pressure.

HIGH ALTITUDE

LOW ALTITUDE

"Just as it takes energy for you to push something (or someone), air **molecules** use up some energy when they push apart. Without as much energy they can't move around as quickly. That's why it is so cold up there," concluded Mr. Moffat.

How Cold Is It? Figure It Out!

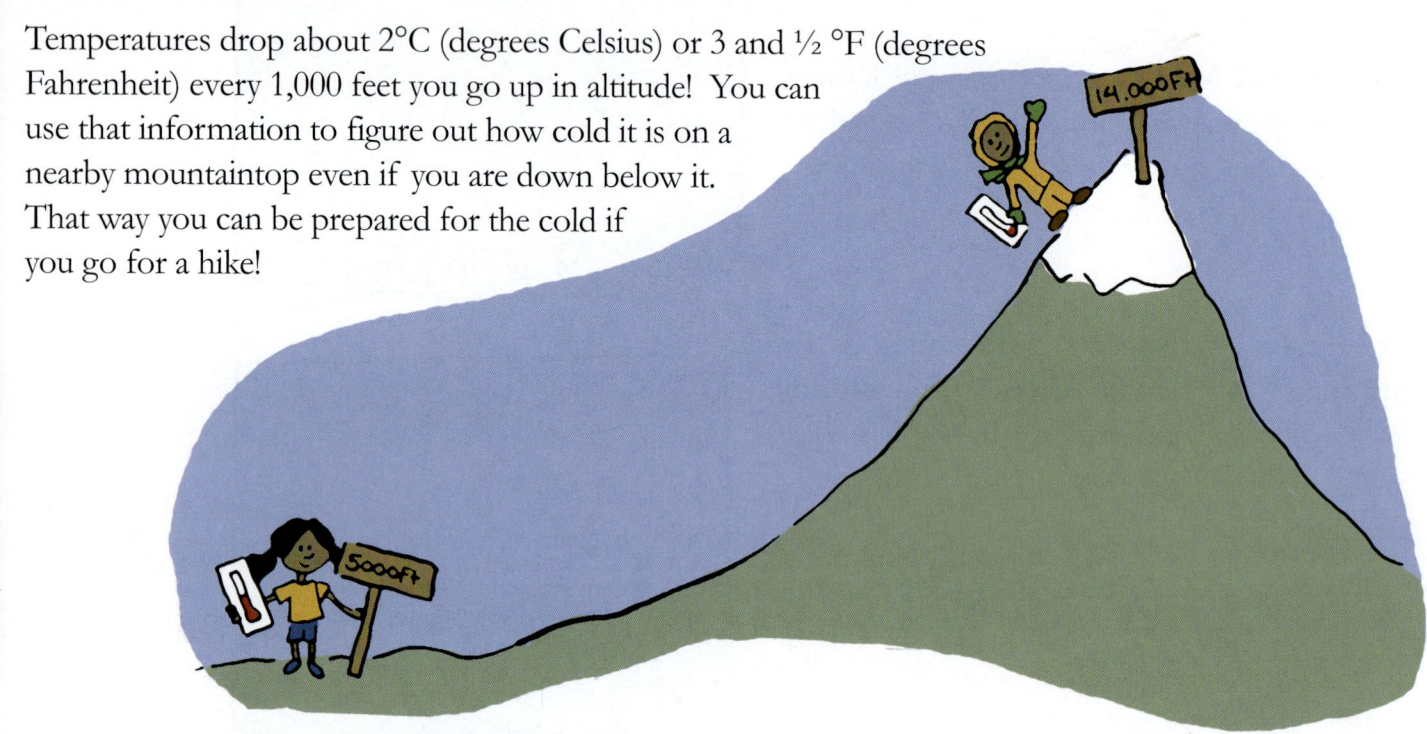

TRY IT!

Temperatures drop about 2°C (degrees Celsius) or 3 and ½ °F (degrees Fahrenheit) every 1,000 feet you go up in altitude! You can use that information to figure out how cold it is on a nearby mountaintop even if you are down below it. That way you can be prepared for the cold if you go for a hike!

Let's say that your town has an **altitude** of 5,000 feet about sea level, and that you are planning a trip to a nearby mountaintop that is about 14,000 feet above sea level.

It is sunny and 20°C (or 68°F) in your town, a nice spring day. But how cold will it be on the top of that mountain?

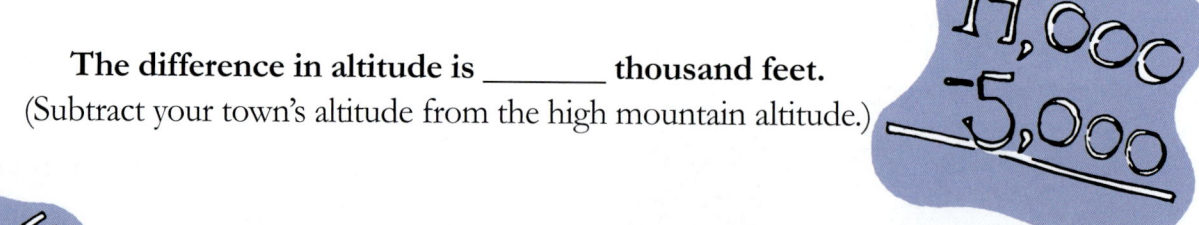

The difference in altitude is _____ thousand feet.
(Subtract your town's altitude from the high mountain altitude.)

$$14{,}000 - 5{,}000$$

The change in temperature is _____ °C.
(A 1,000-foot change in altitude causes a 2°C change in temperature. Multiply the number of thousands of feet that you found above by 2.)

$$9 \times 2 =$$

So, my estimate of the temperature at the top of that mountain is _____ °C.
(Subtract the change in temperature from the temperature of your town.)

$$20 - ?$$

24

TRY IT!

Now that you have figured out the temperature up there, how are you going to protect yourself from the cold when you go on your hike? It might be a little chilly to go hiking up that mountain wearing the same clothes you are wearing at home. Even if it looks like warm weather at lower elevations, remember to take an extra layer of warm clothing with you in your pack!

If you are planning for a hike to a nearby mountain, you can do this calculation to estimate what the temperature might be like. What you will need to know is:

1. The altitude of your town (or a town at the base of the mountain).
2. The temperature forecast for your town (or a town at the base of the mountain).
3. The altitude of the mountain you will be climbing.

Remember that weather is more than just the temperature. Be prepared for rain or snow if it is in the forecast!

Clue #4:
Our Bodies Need Oxygen From Air

He Held His Breath Until Blue in the Face
-by Zachary

"Now that he is two years old, my cousin Martin is pretty cool and definitely a lot more fun to play with. We had fun last weekend playing with all his toys, running around the house, and making a fort under the kitchen table. Then my aunt said it was Martin's bedtime. I told her I could put him in bed."

"Are you sure?" My aunt frowned as she thought about it.

"How hard could it be?" I argued.

"As it turned out, Martin really didn't want to go to bed. He wailed when I tried to get him into his pajamas; he was screaming too loudly to hear when I tried to read his favorite bedtime story; he was still crying when I finally picked him up and put him in his bed.

"I turned to leave the room and suddenly his cries stopped. I turned around; Martin was holding his breath, mad that it was bed time, and he was beginning to turn blue!"

"Come on Martin," I pleaded, "you have to breathe." "I ran around the room tossing toys and stuffed animals into the bed to distract him, I even made funny faces, but he still held his breath. I was out of ideas and just about to run and get my aunt when he started to cry again. Cries might sound bad, but they meant that he was breathing again. I was so relieved. I sunk down to the floor, out of breath myself."

According to Mr. Moffat...
Breathing is Fundamental!

"Well Zachary, while your story is not at all about **altitude**, it does describe an important clue," Mr. Moffat explained thoughtfully as he adjusted his glasses, "that will help us understand how **altitude** affects our bodies.

"All animals need to breath air to survive, even you! The part of the air we need is the **oxygen**.

We exhale the rest of the air **molecules** that we don't need. We also exhale **molecules** of things that our bodies need to get rid of."

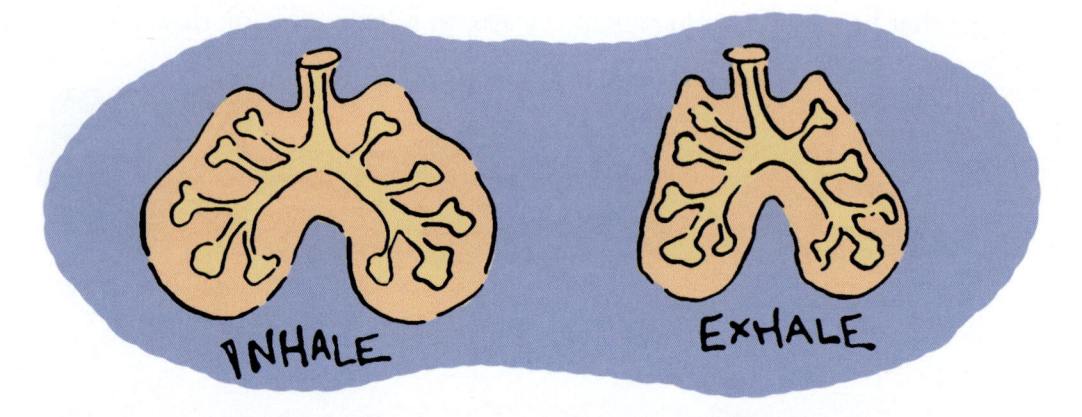

28

"Breathing air is only the first step to getting **oxygen** into places where our bodies need it. **Oxygen** is breathed into the **lungs** with other air **molecules**. Then, in the deepest parts of our **lungs**, small pockets connect the air with little roads where blood races past the **lungs**.

The red parts of the blood pick up **oxygen** from the **lungs** and carry it around the body, from the big toe to the brain.

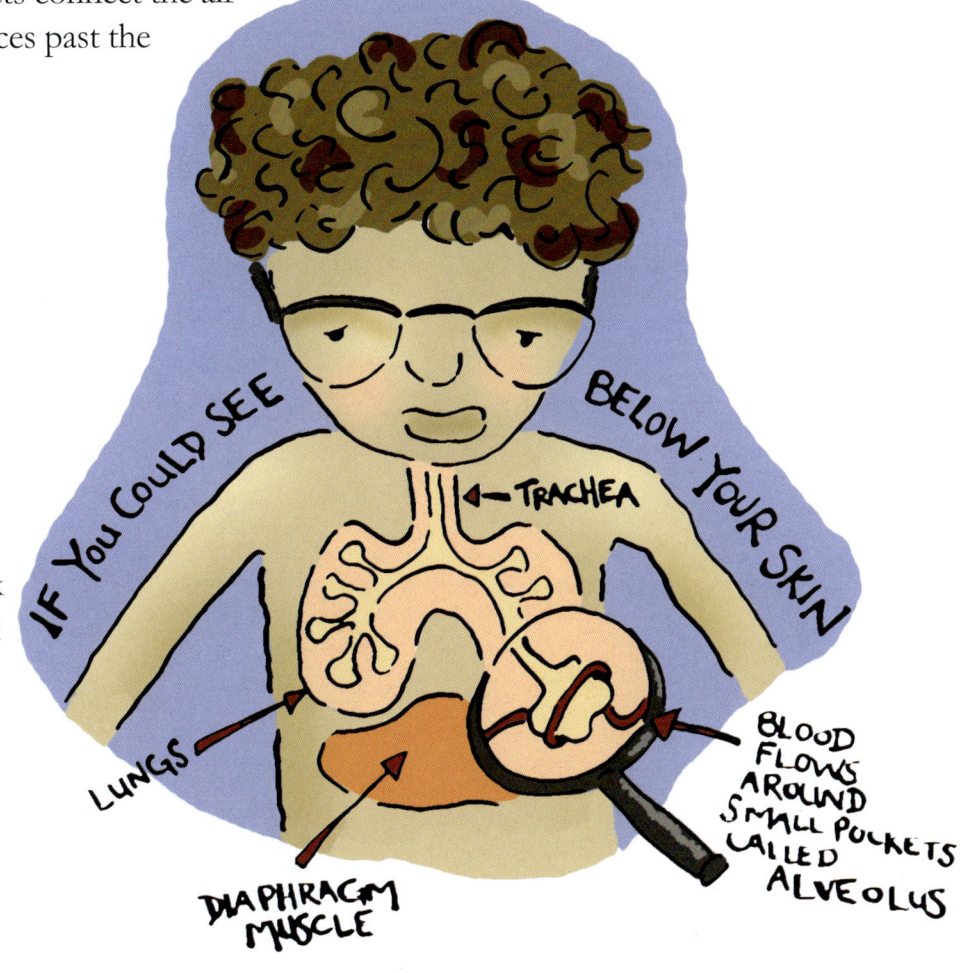

IF YOU COULD SEE BELOW YOUR SKIN
← TRACHEA
LUNGS
DIAPHRAGM MUSCLE
BLOOD FLOWS AROUND SMALL POCKETS CALLED ALVEOLUS

Bodies need **oxygen** to make energy. The energy is used to contract muscles, digest food, and grow larger.

29

Make a Model of Your Lungs!

TRY IT!

Take a big breath of air. Air is going into the **lungs** within your chest. You are breathing all day long without even trying! Ever wonder why the air goes into your **lungs** when you take a breath? You can make a model of your **lungs** to figure out how breathing works!

A model is a small version of something that is enough like the real thing that you can play with it to see how it works. This model is made of very different materials than those that are found within human bodies, but breathing works in a similar way!

What you'll need:

- A 2-liter soda bottle
- Straw
- Modeling clay
- Two large round balloons
- Duct tape
- Two rubber bands

1. Cut off the bottom of the soda bottle. (This will represent the upper body of a person.)

2. Attach the open end of one of the balloons to the straw with a rubber band and secure with duct tape. (This balloon represents the **lungs** and the straw represents the way that air gets into the lungs. People have two lungs, but in this model there will be only one.)

3. Push the straw and attached balloon up through the bottom of the bottle until the straw is in the mouth of the bottle with the balloon below it.

4. Insert modeling clay into the mouth of the bottle so that there is a tight seal.

5. Cut the top narrow part off the second balloon and stretch the wide part over the bottom of the bottle. Secure the balloon over the bottle with a rubber band and duct tape so that there is a tight seal. This balloon represents the **diaphragm muscle** in the model.)

6. Hold the bottle and push the diaphragm balloon up into the soda bottle. Then, pull the diaphragm balloon away from the soda bottle. What happens to the **lung** balloon?

What's Going On?

The **lungs** in your model should inflate and deflate as you push the diaphragm balloon in and out. The **diaphragm** is a muscle. When it moves down, your chest gets bigger and the pressure inside decreases so air rushes into your **lungs** as you inhale. When the **diaphragm** moves up, your chest gets smaller, pressure increases, and air rushes out of your **lungs** as you exhale.

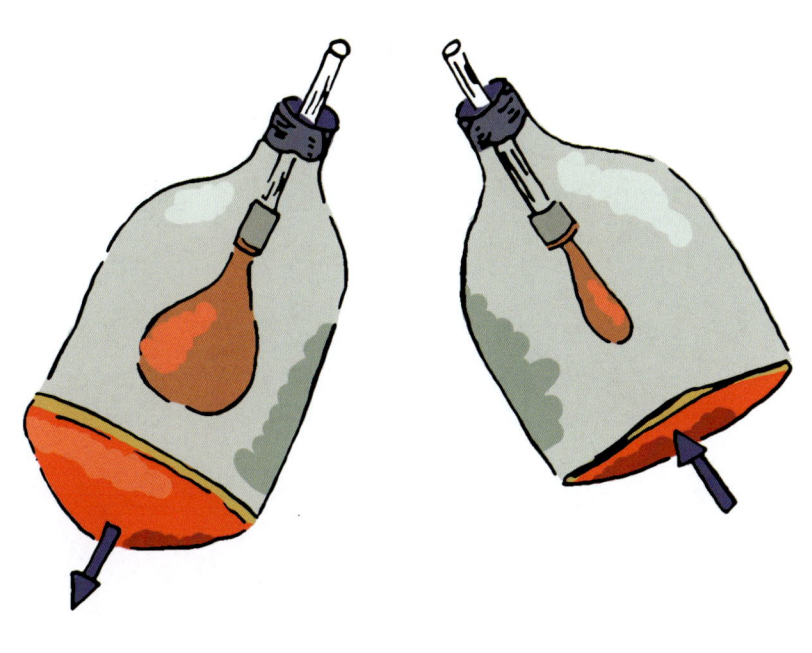

Clue #5: What Happens When a Body Can't Get Enough Oxygen

The Backpacking Trip --
-by Amanda

"My uncle, who lives at the beach, came to visit for a weeklong backpacking trip high in the mountains. We put all the camping gear in the car, picked him up at the airport and drove to the trailhead. We all cheered when we finally saw the sign that said 'Apnea Pass Trailhead, 8,000 ft altitude.'

"Uncle Doug said he had a little headache." "It's probably just from the plane flight!" he chuckled, "I'll take an aspirin if it gets worse." "It did get worse, much worse.

"Uncle Doug is very fit and usually we have trouble keeping up with him, but this time he seemed out of breath all the time and he was clutching his head by the sides as he hiked. He didn't look like he was having a very good time. He complained that his feet were swollen and didn't fit in his hiking boots. I thought that maybe we should stop and let him rest but he wanted to get to our camping spot before the afternoon thunderstorms rolled in.

"We got to our camping spot just before it started to rain. It was really high up on the side of the mountain. Mom and I looked down and saw the road we came in on about 1,500 feet below us. Then we heard Uncle Doug throwing up." "Does he have the flu?" I asked mom. "She looked scared. I turned around to see Uncle Doug and felt pretty scared myself. He looked horrible.

"Uh oh," said mom, "we are going back down right now. He has **altitude sickness**." "We started down the mountain. Luckily, going downhill was easier for him, but he was still stumbling the whole way back to the car.

"I was really worried, but my mom said that we just needed to get him down to a lower **altitude**. About an hour after we got Uncle Doug into the car, we were back at home. He felt tired and had a little headache but was no longer sick.

"Where had the sickness gone? It disappeared as mysteriously as it started."

According to Mr. Moffat…
Altitude Sicknesses Are Different

"Was your uncle ok after that?" asked Monique fearfully.

"Yes. He was fine. It wasn't at all like the flu or a stomachache," replied Amanda.

"That's because germs may be to blame for other sorts of **illnesses**, but they do not cause **altitude sickness**," said Mr. Moffat knowledgeably. "People sometimes become ill at high altitude when their bodies react badly to the lack of **oxygen**. Some illnesses are very mild. Others are very serious. Uncle Doug probably had only a mild **altitude sickness**.

"When you go to high **altitude**, your body tries to adjust to less air **molecules**. Usually, people who live near sea level, like your Uncle Doug, are able to adjust to Colorado's lower **altitudes** without any problems. Most people can also adjust to Colorado's high **altitudes** as well, but it might take a little time. The higher you go, the higher your chance of developing an **altitude sickness**.

"One out of every four people whose bodies are used to living at sea level may feel a little sick when they first get to **altitudes** of 5,000 to 10,000 feet (1,500 to 3,000 meters). People who are used to these **altitudes** might get sick if they go higher. This mild sickness is called **Acute Mountain Sickness**, or **AMS** for short.

"Often the first symptom of **AMS** is a headache, which will go away when your body gets used to the **altitude**.

"Sometimes people feel like they are carsick.

"People often have trouble sleeping when at high **altitudes**.

"To prevent **AMS**, don't go up in altitude too quickly, like Uncle Doug did. During your first two days at a higher **altitude**, take it easy and drink plenty of water to give your body time to adjust. If you take care of yourself and listen to how your body is feeling, it is very unlikely that you will get sick because of the **altitude**. Drinking water and resting or going down to a lower **altitude** may help you to feel better.

"**AMS** is the most common type of **altitude sickness**. It can be very uncomfortable but if you take care of your body, you will be all right."

Get Used to it!

5 Things You can do to Prevent Altitude Sickness

- Don't go up too quickly.
- Take it easy for the first few days.
- Drink plenty of water.
- Eat healthy food.
- Go down lower if you feel sick.

How long can you hold your breath?

TRY IT!

Everyone's body needs **oxygen** to keep going. We breathe to get **oxygen** into our bodies. You don't have to remember to breath. Your body knows when it is time to take another breath. Have you ever wondered how long you can go without breathing? Since everyone is different, some people are able to hold their breath longer than others.

What you'll need:
- A watch with a second hand or a stop watch

1. Take a deep breath and hold it as you start the stopwatch.

2. Stop it when you have to breath again.

Clue #6:
Adapting to Altitude
At the Foot of Mount Everest
-by Jaya

Namaste!
(That's the Sherpa way of saying hello!)

"I am staying in Colorado this year with my Aunt's family, but I usually live in the Khumba Valley of Nepal. From my village, you can see the tall peaks of the Himalayan Mountains. Each year, thousands of people from all over the world come to climb these high mountains, especially the highest mountain on Earth, Mount Everest, whose peak is 29,035 feet above sea level. Many of the travelers don't reach the summits of these huge mountains because they get **altitude sickness**.

"My father says that we Sherpas
have bodies that are adapted to going high.
He works with a team of Sherpas that climbs
high mountains carrying the equipment for expeditions.
Large amounts of equipment are needed to get to the top such as
warm clothing and tents, climbing gear, and tons of food.

"Most climbing expeditions, like those that climb Everest, rely on Sherpas to
help them carry the gear. I'm only 10 years old, but someday I hope to climb
Mount Everest too."

According to Mr. Moffat...

People Can Get Used to the Altitude

"Some people's families have lived in high **altitude** places for hundreds of years, like Jaya's family in the mountains of Nepal. These people have bodies that are prepared for high **altitude**. Their **lungs** are larger so that they can take in more air with each breath. They are able to breathe faster too.

Mount Everest 29,035 ft.

"Even if you just live at **altitude** for a short time, your body will get used to living with less **oxygen**. You will not be able to develop the adaptations that the Sherpa people have, but your body will try to get used to the new conditions.

"You might find that you breathe quickly..

"...and your heart beats faster.

"Your heart and your lungs have to do more work when you are at high altitude because there is less **oxygen**. They work hard to get **oxygen** to all parts of your body"

Make Mountain Prayer Flags

TRY it!

For hundreds of years people in Tibet and Nepal have hung special flags in places that are important to them. Many people take prayer flags to Mount Everest and other high mountains in the Himalayas. Written on the flags are symbols that indicate the hopes and dreams of the person who hung them.

What you'll need:

- Pieces of cloth (8˝ x 8˝ squares or larger)
- Markers
- String
- Craft glue, clothespins, or small binder clips

1. Think about the things that are important to you such as your hopes for your friends, family and the people of the world. Draw and write your hopes on the flag. According to Tibetan traditions, your hopes will be carried by the wind to people and places around the world.

2. Cut a piece of string long enough to hold all the prayer flags.

3. Fold the top of each flag over the string and secure it with glue, clothespins, or small binder clips.

4. Hang the string with prayer flags somewhere that is special to you.

The bell rang right as they were hanging their prayer flags all over the room.

"Well! I've learned a lot today," said Abby Brittlefern as she clipped her flag to a string. "I guess you have all had enough experience with mountains and high altitudes. So, you probably wouldn't want go on a fieldtrip to the mountains with me," she said trying to hide her smile.

Nobody wanted to be left behind, so the whole class and Mr. Moffat went on a expedition with Abby Brittlefern to Grays Peak. They hiked, picnicked, took pictures, met some wildlife, and remembered something else about high altitude places...

It's fun up here!

On your next trip to the mountains...

1. Pack Clothing for cool temperatures.
2. Pay attention to how you are feeling.
3. Make sure other people in your group feel healthy.
4. Drinks lots of water.
5. Have Fun!
6. Appreciate the AIR around you!

Glossary

Acute Mountain Sickness - Acute Mountain Sickness is an illness that can affect people who go to altitudes (above 8,000 feet) too quickly. It happens when a person's body does not react well to the lower air pressure and lower concentration of oxygen found at higher altitudes.

Adaptation - Adaptations are changes that happen over many generations to make a group of people, plants, or other living things, better able to tolerate conditions in the environment. For instance, over hundreds of years, the Sherpas have developed lungs that are well adapted to the high altitude environment in which they live.

Air Pressure - Air pressure depends on the frequency of collisions between molecules in the air. When air molecules are packed closely together, they collide more often, and Pressure is high. When air molecules are spread further apart, they collide less often, and pressure is low. The weight of the air above causes air pressure to be higher at sea level than on high mountaintops.

Altitude - Altitude is the distance about sea level (the surface of the sea). It tells you how high a place is. For Instance, the altitude of Denver, Colorado, is 5,280 feet (one mile!).

Altitude Sickness (AMS) - A condition caused by a lack of adaptation to high altitudes. The symptoms of altitude sickness include headache, fatigue, shortness of breath, nausea, unsteadiness and dizziness, loss of appetite, insomnia, weakness, and in rare cases, seizures and coma. Different people have different susceptibilities to altitude sickness.

Atmosphere - The atmosphere surrounding our planet is made of a mixture of gases such as oxygen and nitrogen that we call air. The molecules of gasses become farther apart the farther you travel from the Earth's surface. The atmosphere is very important for living things. Animals need to breath it, plants take molecules from it as they make their own food, and it blocks dangerous rays from the sun.

Diaphragm Muscle - The diaphragm muscle is important for respiration. When you contract your diaphragm muscle, your lungs are able to take air in as you inhale. You exhale when your diaphragm muscle relaxes.

Gravity - When you drop something, it falls because of gravity! Gravity is a force of attraction between all things. The object you dropped is attracted towards the earth so it falls!

Lungs - The lungs bring air and blood into close contact so that oxygen can be added to the blood and waste, like carbon dioxide, can be taken away.

Molecule - A molecule is the smallest portion of substance. You can't see individual molecules. For instance, if you had a molecule of broccoli on your dinner place, you wouldn't even know it was there, but you could see many, many broccoli molecules together! A molecule is usually made of several tiny parts called atoms that are stuck together.

Nitrogen - Most of our atmosphere is made of molecules of nitrogen gas. Each nitrogen gas molecule is made of two atoms of nitrogen that are stuck together. Nitrogen is also a part of the molecules that make up your body, other animals bodies, and plants.

Oxygen - Oxygen is commonly found as a colorless gas that makes up about 20% of earth's atmosphere. Animals need to breath oxygen to survive.

Resources for Educators and Other Curious People!

Ardley, Neil. The Science Book of Air. Toronto: Doubleday Canada Ltd., 1991.

Krakauer, Jon. Into Thin Air, A Personal Account of the Mount Everest Disaster: Anchor Books, 1998.

Everest: The Death Zone, NOVA Video
An extensive look a what happens to human bodies once they enter the high altitude "death zone" of Mount Everest. Though scientifically fascinating, the graphic nature of the film may be disturbing to some audiences.

NOVA Online Everest Web Site
The companion to the NOVA Death Zone video, this web site offers more information about altitude and the people who have climbed the world's highest mountain.
http://www.pbs.org/wgbh/nova/everest

Windows to the Universe
An extensive educational resource for people of all ages to explore our world, our solar system, and Universe. Visit the Teacher Resources section to discover a wealth of hands-on activities appropriate for K-12 classrooms.
http://www.windows.ucar.edu

The National Center for Atmospheric Research
A wealth of information about the atmosphere, weather and climate. Special sections for kids describe concepts of atmospheric science with colorful graphics and games. The Educators' Bridge contains a wealth of resources for teachers including curriculum and access to digital libraries.
http://www.eo.ucar.edu/

Resources for Educators and Other Curious People!

Using this book in the classroom:
We invite teachers to use the stories, science, activities and experiments in this book in their classrooms! The National Science Education Standards that correlate with different sections of this book are listed below.

Part 1: What is Air
Content Standard A: Science as Inquiry
Content Standard B: Physical Science
Content Standard D: Earth and Space Science

Part 2: Air Pressure and Altitude
Content Standard A: Science as Inquiry
Content Standard B: Physical Science
Content Standard D: Earth and Space Science

Part 3: Low Air Pressure Makes it Cold!
Content Standard B: Physical Science
Content Standard D: Earth and Space Science

Part 4: Our Bodies Need Oxygen From Air
Content Standard C; Life Science

Part 5: What Happens When a Body Can't Get Enough Oxygen
Content Standard A: Science as Inquiry
Content Standard C: Life Science
Content Standard F: Science in Personal and Social Perspectives

Part 6: Adapting to Altitude
Content Standard F: Science in Personal and Social Perspectives